NO AVOIDING IT

NO AVOIDING IT

NEIL FULWOOD

All rights reserved. No part of this work covered by the copyright herein may be reproduced or used in any means – graphic, electronic, or mechanical, including copying, recording, taping, or information storage and retrieval systems – without written permission of the publisher.

Printed by imprintdigital
Upton Pyne, Exeter
www.digital.imprint.co.uk

Typesetting and cover design by narrator
www.narrator.me.uk
info@narrator.me.uk
033 022 300 39

Published by Shoestring Press
19 Devonshire Avenue, Beeston, Nottingham, NG9 1BS
(0115) 925 1827
www.shoestringpress.co.uk

First published 2017
© Copyright: Neil Fulwood

The moral right of the author has been asserted.

© Copyright author photo: Dennis Apple

© Copyright front cover collage: Mini van by Dave Fulwood; AEC Mercury by Janet Fulwood; Hickings Pentecost Building and Trent House by Neil Fulwood; Bestwood colliery headstocks by Sue Paterson.

ISBN 978-1-910323-72-4

ACKNOWLEDGEMENTS

Some of these poems, or earlier versions of them, originally appeared in:

Alliterati, Amaryllis, Ancient Heart, Art Decades, The Black Light Engine Room, The Camel Saloon, Dead Snakes, FourCulture, International Times, The Interpreter's House, The Lampeter Review, Leaves of Ink, LeftLion, London Grip, Lunar Poetry, Medusa's Kitchen, The Morning Star, Nottingham Drinker, The Ofi Press, The Screech Owl, Uneven Floor, VerseWrights and *The Writers' Hub.*

'Exit' was inspired by a painting by Ira Lightman, who also advised on redrafting the poem.

My thanks to Viv Apple, Ross Bradshaw, Ruth Fainlight, Martin Figura, Helen Ivory, John Lucas, Roy Marshall, Carl Sharpe and David Sillitoe; and to family, friends and comrades.

For Paula, with love

CONTENTS

THAT WAS THEN, THIS IS NOW
    Sepia   3
    Pit Bus   4
    Whatever Happened   5
    Exit   6
    Trailer Tent   7
    Home Town   8
    Family Business   11
    Depot   12
    Not by Landmarks but Street Names   13
    Wild One   14
    Forecourt, 11PM   15
    Bank Holiday   16

WORK IS THE CURSE …
    No Avoiding It   21
    The Expletive Deleted of the Average Briton   22
    Last of the Famous International Nobodies   23
    The Usual Suspects   24
    Data Entry   26
    The Art of Killing Time   27
    Nobody Ever Says Thank You   28
    Personal Improvement Plan   29
    Dear Lord, I Pray   30
    The Sausage That Killed Capitalism   31

… OF THE DRINKING CLASSES
    Honest Piss   37
    Silver Ball   38
    All-Dayer   39
    Offer   42
    Irish Bar, East Midlands   43
    Carmelita   44
    The Long Dark Chucking-Out Time of the Soul   45
    Litany   47
    Last Orders at the Jerusalem Tavern   50

That was then, this is now

SEPIA

The last memory you have of him,
you were nine: his chair angled
toward the fire, hands unsteady
at the business of cup and saucer.
He'd shrunk into himself; seemed
less. He paused between breaths.

Today you're scanning photos
and he's younger than you –
a bullish twenty-something
in pinstripe and thin tie,
wearing a hat with the élan
of a mobster or movie star,

one bulky fist clutching a pint,
the other unfolding a V-sign
to the camera, cigarette burning
in the centre of it. There's a look
about him as if a girl or a fight
is how the evening's playing out.

Even cooler: this snapshot of him
astride a Norton, leather gloves,
bomber jacket, motorcycle goggles,
hair slicked back. Crash helmet?
He'd laugh and gun the throttle,
call you daft that you worry so much.

PIT BUS

My father as a boy of eight or nine
in a stern woman's house, hands
that preferred Meccano doing bored injustice
to an upright piano. Hands itching
for the real business of a truck engine.

Scales, rudimentary tunes, *Für Elise*
hammered out like a panel-beaten dent.
My father yawning, the metronome
chopping away at his attention span,
eyes drifting from the keys

to the mirror on the parlour wall.
The pit bus passing meant it was done,
the lesson he took nothing from, that hour
of enforced respectability. My father,
free to take the long way home

while winding gear lurched out
the held-breath sound of a cage
descending. Darkness, dust. Men
spitting out phlegm and profanity,
the shift beginning.

WHATEVER HAPPENED

I can't trust my memories. Last year
is a fuzzy question mark, never mind
the landscape of a decade
without internet or mobile phones.

Someone jammed a breeze block
on the IT accelerator and stunt-dived
out of the '80s, leaving them ploughing
towards the millennium. You've seen

the movie: a disaster epic with a cast
of thousands, most of them uncredited
as collateral damage. A quantum leap
from the '70s that I think I remember

(we didn't have a colour TV till '76
or maybe later) though I can't be sure,
looking back from a plateau
of social media, whether the images

I'm slapping in the face of the present
have been signed off as accurate
or revealed as an identikit collage
of flares, sideburns and Hillman Hunters,

Jack Regan and working men's pubs,
Bob and Terry and beer and birds
and the sense even then of change
in the air. I can't trust my memories.

I suspect the feeling's mutual.

EXIT

They have become sharp with each other,
this young couple – bored, cold, out
of pocket, each seeking to nail down
whose brilliant idea it was:

three tickets to the circus, splintery stalls,
the smell of assorted animals
and their leavings; routines
rolled-out for the umpteenth time.

And their child demanding exit,
dragged through the audience
screaming, head-shake defiant
against going back in.

A truce of pursed lips and rolled eyes.
Handbag-fished tissue blots tears,
small clenched hands find theirs.
Then the drive home, the big-top smaller

than a wind-up toy in the rearview mirror
and their boy steeling himself
for nightmares of sawdust and a dark circle
seething with the faces of clowns.

TRAILER TENT

The theory was sound: holidays
as *ad hoc* adventurism, trailer hooked
to the back of the car and off
where the fancy took us. In practice

it was two summers of steady rain.
Canvas sagged. Sludge bubbled
under groundsheets. We staved off cold
with a Calor-Gas stove, filled the tent

with thin aromas of tinned goods.
Spaghetti hoops or alphabet soup
in plastic bowls. Sleep was dictated
by voices outside, unidentified lights.

Mornings we packed it all away, yawning
through a ritual of folding and stowing
everything flat under the tonneau cover.
A busman's holiday for my father

the truck driver, a scaled-down version
of roping and sheeting. Maybe
that's what sealed its fate. The last place
we pitched it was the back garden.

Decades before eBay it went just as quickly,
bills changing hands, the forecast improving.

HOME TOWN

This is where I have found myself:
middle aged and already digging
an escape tunnel of memory
back to the '70s – decades too late,
even then, for me to get away with
any of that "it was all fields here"

crap. What it was around here
was streets and terraces and beer-offs
you could still get tuppence back
on empty bottles. What it was
was roads that weren't snarled
with traffic and a Raleigh bike

you rode without kneepads or
helmet, down to the level crossing,
gated and watched over
by a signal box like a sniper's nest;
you counted the wagons, all of them
heaped with coal and taken for granted.

Or you rode in the other direction
past St Mary's, along Main Street
with its glass-fronted shops
and up toward the industrial estate,
a row of uneven units and factories,
bodyshops and trade counters

and precision-turned parts. The places
your dad or your uncle worked.
These are the places I find myself
thinking about. The open-plan offices
I blagged myself into on three GCEs
are environs I'm steadily falling

away from, their paperless protocols
a monkey-pole blueprint for corporate
climbers half my age. I'm done;
it's down to luck or restructuring
whether retirement or redundancy
pin the bullseye on me first.

Too late, anyway: I've found myself
stooping to pick up the mantle
of those old guys in the pub
I used to despair of, the "back in my day"
brigade, the "when I wor a lad" whingers,
the flat-capped old-timers I thought of

as low-rent versions of the Ancient
Mariner, older and wiser and ready
to stop you with a checklist of reasons
why you were wrong and shouldn't
do it. Now I'm joining in, enumerating
the pubs and shops and meeting places

boarded up and bulldozed and fenced
off for demolition. The hardware shop
you'd go to for eyelets, nails, screws,
lightbulbs, lengths of copper wire, tools;
it's now a Greggs. The family-owned
newsagents who measured out sweets

on old-fashioned scales and sold
magic tricks and jokes and maintained
a revolving wire rack of paperbacks
near the door that anyone could have
grabbed from and made a run for it
but no-one did. It's now a chain

and the cashier asks if you need
a mobile phone top-up. I'm on contract,
haven't had a landline in a decade

but set a pint before me, point me
in the direction of the recent past
and I'll recall the Bakelite phone,

a finger jabbed through drilled-out
Perspex, dragging the dial
to its furthest extent. Never mind
the iPhone I've allowed to dictate
to me – internet, email, facetime
and apps – there was something

in the slow conjuration of a number
that anchored the simple act
of calling a friend, cast it as ritual,
something expensive and not just done
to hear someone's voice.
Cameras were SLRs and pricey

or Polaroids spewing slabs of plastic
yanked from the slit and flicked into life,
lens flare squares confined to albums
and the fading shelf-life of cut-rate nostalgia.
I don't bother with photos now, recoil
from the instant-memory culture

of meeting friends at Wetherspoons
or the coffee bar and two hours later
uploading to Facebook a dozen pictures.
Kids young enough to be my kids
watching concerts through the screen
of the mobile device they're recording it on.

This is where I've found myself:
middle aged and tunnelling back
to *The Sweeney* and gatefold LPs,
when a tanned leather jacket
was a sign you'd made it; a Ford
Cortina meant the world was yours.

FAMILY BUSINESS

Weekends were maintenance and balancing
the books. Saturdays we got our hands dirty.
The cab tilted to check tappet clearances.
A crawlboard under the chassis, back aching.

Latching up wheelnuts, a length of steel tubing
slipped onto the torque-wrench
for leverage, knuckles white through the dirt
as it groaned then clicked in confirmation:

did six-hundred newton metres
mean they were good and tight? I don't remember.
I didn't have a head for the technical side.
Sundays were my forte: clean hands and sheets

of paper, the columns of figures easy enough
before spreadsheets and pull-throughs
and look-ups confused accounting.
Now in the office I'm almost innumerate

compared to the whiz-kids.
Back then I was fifteen and doing the invoicing
for a one-man-firm with a sixteen tonner,
tapping numbers into an old-school calculator,

its spool of paper chattering out the profit and loss,
a ticker-tape parade if we weren't in the red.

DEPOT

It hangs there on a sign
lettered in the Seventies,
a word with a fag in its mouth:

depot. A word redolent
of oily patches on broken concrete
and a row of lorries

parked against a clapboard structure.
Tea from a flask, dregs flicked out.
A makeshift shelf stacked with box files

in an office that'd be happier
as a workshop. Punch clock
and girlie calendar, walls

painted in leftover green.
Some vital support service
ticking away in the background.

NOT BY LANDMARKS BUT STREET NAMES

The man on the bus is talking to himself.
In a voice nuanced as a hold message, he names
the streets of whatever map his mind is traversing –
Curzon Street, Meadow Lane, Harrow Road.

Odd route, leapfrogging city centre and river,
swerving round the football ground
to creep through the suburbs; a mind-map
folded like a paper plane. Were these streets

the geography of his rites of passage,
streets he walked in flares and scuffed trainers
or bundled into scarf and coat
for that first father-son trip to Meadow Lane,

his dad glaring at the blokes effing and blinding
to the side and behind them, a grunted "mind the lad";
or does he work these streets now, sweeping
fag ends and wrappers. Does he name them

as a wood carver, running his hand the length
of the grain, would name pine and linden and grey ash;
name them as a man who has known his city on foot,
who does not shirk from lowered car windows

and requests for directions; who navigates
not by landmarks but street names.

WILD ONE

Labouring in low gear
up a slope heavy with snow

I get a half-second snapshot
of full-throttle joy. A man

taking the downhill path
on a mobility scooter

like a slalom, grinning
under hat and scarf, coat

blown back by the wind –
cool as a pirate or private eye

– and I still don't know
if his tee-shirt said Motörhead

or Black Sabbath, just
that he blipped from the rearview

as if through a wormhole
while I took ten minutes

over the two blocks home,
driving carefully.

FORECOURT, 11PM

Nothing like that Edward Hopper painting
with the old guy locking up the pumps
at a rural gas station, the bruise of sunset
behind the treeline. No, this is the forecourt

at 11PM, half a mile from the city centre:
concrete, floodlights, a fuel company logo
no-one would bother committing to canvas.
It's more like the set of a cheap sci-fi movie,

production design wonky and unconvincing,
light and shadow refusing to correlate.
Thunderbird 2's guzzling unleaded, pod
loaded with pizzas and a fuckton of beer.

The Millennium Falcon's been running on fumes,
three figures on the pump to brim the tank.
The Mekon drives a pimped flying saucer,
drum 'n' bass and a Playboy sticker. He's

wearing shades despite the hour. His eyes
are like piss-holes in the surface of Venus.

BANK HOLIDAY

May has got its act together
and rolled a sunny weekend
off the production line, thumbing
its nose at April's cold snaps
and squalls, leaving it
to its *cruellest month* reputation.

The estate celebrates.
Lawnmowers and strimmers gang up
against eardrums. Beer-bellied men
wield cheap power tools
as if they were felling trees
in British Columbia. Hangover?

Hayfever? Hoping for a lie-in
and a quiet morning? Screw you:
these are men on a mission, men
who dream of Harley-Davidsons
and the open road, never mind
they couldn't balance a Lambretta.

Men brandishing hedge trimmers
like it's an X-box shoot-up,
who never came closer to the theatre
of conflict than watching *Saving
Private Ryan* half a dozen times
on the big screen; who've agreed

over the haze of an unexploded barbecue
that bringing back National Service
is what these little bastards need.
Ah yes, the barbeque: it's waiting
to inscribe the Hollywood burnish
of the evening sky with the lazy

charcoal smudge of its signature;
waiting to cue a dozen radios
into disharmony; waiting to chug
its clinging reek over the estate,
urging you back inside, windows
emphatically shut, rooms stifling.

Work is the curse ...

NO AVOIDING IT

It's Sunday evening, pushing midnight, and what's left
in the wine bottle is apportioning itself
into the early stretches of Monday morning. It's 1AM
and there's another chapter to read or the depths
of freeview to explore and there's always
Jack Daniels or Southern Comfort by way of a nightcap.
It's dark and your toe seeks out hard surfaces
to stub itself on, anything and everything
between the bedroom and the kitchen; it's somewhere
between late and early and your throat is sandpaper
without a lath of wood to fetch up to smoothness;
the glass throws itself from the cupboard, the tap
finds a way to dispense cold water like a bullet.

Then it's the time you set the alarm for and you curse
your clock or mobile for making it personal –
grudges held on both sides, the Hatfields and McCoys
squaring off along the dusty main street
of Monday morning, the saloon way behind you
and the loaded gun of the working week
drawn faster than you could ever match, cocked
and levelled, the single eye of its barrel
staring you down, and not even the whistle
of a train in the distance, not even the chance
of something taking you away. Away from all of this.

THE EXPLETIVE DELETED OF THE AVERAGE BRITON

> "The average Briton swears fourteen times a day."
> – from an article in THE METRO

The first as your fist deals with the alarm –
make that two if you wake with a hangover.
The stubbed toe or the elbow impacting
on the dado rail's chamfered corner -
that'll be the second or third, depending.

Spilled coffee? Minor oath. Dropped toast
executing that mid-air flip to ensure
its buttery side smears the kitchen floor? Oath
in B Major. The gridlock and frayed nerves
of the drive to work? Horn Concerto in F.

The office threatens a grand symphony,
a Mahlerian parade of missed promotions
and belligerent bosses, rendered
in the arpeggios of Anglo-Saxon, four letters
to the word as surely as beats to the bar;

but you hold back. You're in the arena
of best behaviour, the all-hearing ear
of the conference call attuned to even
the softest imprecation. Thought-profanity
replaces the verbal, Orwell in Dilbert's cubicle.

Does it count as one of your fourteen
if it's imagined – a word bubbling
into being in the mind's alphabet soup,
the four syllables of what you think of your boss
achieving their Oedipal rendezvous?

LAST OF THE FAMOUS INTERNATIONAL NOBODIES

At the office, he cuts his opinions loose
and sends them scuttling between
desks and filing cabinets. Before he goes
home, he retrieves them from the bins,

dusts them off, locks them in a drawer
ready for tomorrow.
God forbid he'd have nothing to bore
his colleagues with; God forbid he'd go

home and feed those endless evening hours
into the grinder of allotment and DIY
and not rely on it being within his power
to have a voice again at work. The sky

self-harms: bleeds sunset. He's still awake,
trying to place that quote about the bars
two men stare out of (Wilde? Byron? Blake?):
one of 'em sees mud and one stars.

Surely some mistake? Surely it's not that
clear cut? How about this: one man
looks through the window of a studio flat
and turns away, denies the reflection's him.

THE USUAL SUSPECTS

I'm pretending to read on lunch break,
finding cover behind the covers, crimping
the spine between thumb and finger,

holding these three hundred pages
of dog-eared second-handness
just high enough to maintain the illusion.

My eyes flicker like an assassin's, leaping
from page to person. I'm pretending to read
while I review the cast of characters

populating the whole soap opera
of office politics. The helpdesk techies,
upgrading sitcom cliché to truism;

the HR crew with their knowing looks
and files on everyone, the J. Edgars
of the third floor; Sales in shirtsleeves,

ties louder than their mouths, brash
as a coachload of footie fans,
an away fixture and a ruck on the cards.

The car park attendant, in from the cold
of his wooden hut, hands curled
round a cup of tea. The corporate wannabe,

laptop and latte, shooting envious glances
at the fat suits with the Mercs and perks:
the crème de la corpulence of senior management,

the Head of This and Director of That,
Executive Something in Charge of Whatever,
with their blue-sky thinking and KPIs

and all the things they benchmark against.
And the cards they mark when it's time
to downsize. To hell with it. I turn a page

and lower my eyes. My book
is a better lunchtime companion,
full of violence, deceit and ulterior motives.

DATA ENTRY

His fingers bash at the keyboard,
needing no thought to guide them.
The pile of forms on his desk
are leaves blowing through the forest

of his mind. Trudging deeper
into the metaphor, the fallen trees
of his motivation are thick with moss
and there's a rank stench floating up

from the mulch of his career path.
The snail of his clock-watching
inches painfully across the few feet
of the working day, while the squirrel

of his early-doors dash to the pub
is almost a blur, zipping from trunk
to branch. The scrabble of its claws
like fingers on a keyboard.

THE ART OF KILLING TIME

Shuffle papers. Jot meaningfully on a blotter
or notepad – a flurry of words punctuated
by thoughtful pauses. Have several browsers open

like the panels in a triptych; flip between them,
minimise and restore in different orders.
Pull files from cabinets. Take your time

putting them back. Be methodical. Be slow.
Go through reports from previous quarters.
Compare something with something else.

Dial internal numbers that don't exist. Sigh
and tut and drag out the minutes till you hang up.
Diarise. Forward plan. Update distribution lists.

Jot meaningfully. Shuffle papers. Punctuate
with thoughtful pauses. Pull files. Dial
internal numbers. Hope nobody answers.

NOBODY EVER SAYS THANK YOU

Desk-shackled thirty-seven and a half hours
a week. Colleagues drift outside for fag breaks
who don't even smoke. Absenteeism
totals more work days lost than points in a game
of *Words with Friends* if you played it
as a triple word, "B" placed on a triple letter.

Your sanity break: the iPhone's colourful clamour
of games downloaded for free. Until
the Deputy Team Leader catches you at it
and mouths off ahead of next month's appraisal.
Your granddad would have quit the factory for less
and decked the prick on his way out.

A smidge under the living wage for this:
keying in customer comments, hitting save
on half-hearted homilies, trending the tendency
of the general public to rely on parrot-like phrases:
What did we do well? Everything. *What
could we have done better?* Nothing. *Which

member of staff made your visit memorable?*
Not you, friend; not the data entry clerk
marginally less well regarded than the guy
who replenishes the water cooler, hoisting
those outsized plastic containers, latching
them in place, upside down and gurgling out

the air bubble cascade of a drowning man.

PERSONAL IMPROVEMENT PLAN

So here we are. This is where a sense of humour
and ambivalence to the internet use policy
has got me. I would like to thank Oscar Wilde,
Dorothy Parker, Lenny Bruce and Bill Hicks
for showing me the way. I would like to thank
Facebook, Buzzfeed and IMDb for using my time
productively. To every meme and e-card
on the internet, a debt of gratitude. To every
website that traffics in NSFW, a tip of the hat.

So here we are, me and some guy in a bad suit,
some guy who's never read Dostoyevsky
or seen a film by Werner Herzog, who doesn't
know Monet from a Google doodle, who never
rose as part of a standing ovation after Haitink
conducted Beethoven's 9th. Me and some guy
who speaks in TLAs, his job title stanchioned
with the word "manager". *That* guy. I sneak
a glance at my watch when I know he's looking.

DEAR LORD, I PRAY

There will be peace in the valley
and hosannas on the hillside,
there will be calm in the meadow
and a place in the cool declivities
where the carnivore will lie down
with the main course, where
the snake and the mongoose
will contemplate an existence
undefined by killing each other.

It will come at the cost of chaos
in business parks and vicious acts
the likes of which training rooms
can only imagine. It will come
at the cost of souls leeched out
during orientation sessions.
Behind every meeting request,
the eyeless shadow of a cowl
and the thin blade of a scythe.

THE SAUSAGE THAT KILLED CAPITALISM

for David

Like a movie half remembered
from a midnight screening –
a weird blend of *Eat Drink Man Woman*
and *I'm All Right, Jack* – it begins

with our hero getting in early one morning,
setting up a hob in the staff canteen,
frying a small but respectable breakfast.
Grassed up by the Health & Safety bod

he shrugs off the foreman's question
Why not have breakfast at home?
as something not worth answering.
The explanation he'd pull from the bag

if pressed would be: *Alarm rings at six,
showered by half past, here for seven.
Not hungry that early, but starving
long before lunch.* If pressed he'd liken

that stab of hunger to a lifelong dipso
waiting out his first drink – waiting it out
on point of principle – till the sun's
over the yardarm. But he's not pressed.

By now, he's providing breakfast cobs
to order: bacon and sausage
from a friend of a friend of a local farmer;
freshly laid eggs with the compliments

of an old lady who still keeps hens,
a sort-of aunt who once killed pigs
and stirred their blood so it didn't congeal,
who didn't waste a single part of the animal,

whose black pudding was the stuff
of legend. The shop floor lads offer money
(the office wallahs are less forthcoming)
but he waves away their loose change

and the occasional crumpled five pound note
but accepts if it's offered after work
a pint of ale or double whisky. Accepts
a free haircut from a colleague's brother

who runs a barber's shop – a proper
old-fashioned enterprise, 1970s Brylcreem ads
framed on the wall and a pole
with its red and white alternations

spiralling outside the premises. Accepts
a pre-MOT service *gratis* from a guy
in the welding bay who occasionally moonlights
for a family-owned garage. Accepts

a bottle of homemade elderberry wine
from Fiona in accounts whose grandfather
hailed from the Highlands, who could rig up
a still in her spare room if she wanted.

Slowly the mindset of favour-for-favour
and payment-in-kind makes its way through
sales office into the boardroom. Clients collecting
their however-much of whatever-it-is

this firm manufactures enjoy a free fry up
as their van's loaded. Pretty soon
delivery costs cease to factor. Jeff in contracts
diversifies into seminars aimed at

facilitating a small business collective;
our hero provides the brunch menu
as attendees get the message (the sausage
cob is ever-popular). Contracts are won

on the strength of a breakfast buffet,
and PowerPoint presentations
are soon shrugged off as mere set dressing.
Quotes scribbled on the back of a napkin

make pie charts and columns of figures redundant.
Business gets done like it's the '50s
and no lousy bastard's invented logistics:
a gentleman's agreement closed by a handshake.

It takes root: an idea, an alternative –
quid pro quo and quality of service,
customer loyalty, investment in staff;
it tests that its root is firm and then

crosses time zones and language barriers,
the *entente cordiale* of the stomach
greeting delegates with bread and cheese
and meat and wine, the table set

for friends of all appetites and ages;
then takes leave of the dinner table
while toasts are made and friendships forged,
trusting to the *amuse bouche* of the appetisers

and the hearty fare of the main course
to seal the deal while it throws wider the net
of its purpose, a statement of intent
couched in the language of the underpaid

and the underfed, its groundswell inviting
stock market fixation on unfloated companies
with interests in culinary-exchange trading,
a clamour denied by worldwide refusal

(on general principle) of all members
of the breakfast cob collective. Bankers
struggle to comprehend it. Wall Street
takes a hit and takes umbrage. Lawyers falter,

the precedent dubious on legal action
where a breakfast cob is the named defendant.
Business finds in favour of the little guy
who plays fair and pays his taxes –

a success story that amplifies its own epicentre,
sends out shockwaves that dislodge yen and dollar,
casting them down to the depths
of the dreary old pound; shockwaves

that set off a thousand flashbulbs,
the covers of Forbes and Newsweek
and Time magazine imprinted with images
of those at the forefront of the new economy:

bratwurst, salami, chorizo, kielbasa,
saveloy, black pudding, Lincolnshire sausage.

... of the drinking classes

HONEST PISS

Remember the Seventies? A decade
of muted colours: gunmetal greys, browns like rust.
Everywhere dark interiors: amusement arcades,
pool halls, cinemas. Pubs – spit 'n' sawdust

archetypes. Linoleum floors. No frills. Back then,
no curved metallic pumps: the choice
was bitter or mild. Lager was for girls. In Nottingham
you drank Home Ales or Shipstones

(Shippoes or if you rearranged the letters
"honest piss") – it was like supporting Forest or
County, listening to disco or punk.

Now it's wall-to-wall carpeting, wine lists, feta
cheese and humus. Do you miss the spit 'n' sawdust, the simple honesty of getting drunk?

SILVER BALL

He's dragged a barstool
in front of the quiz machine
and neglected his pint,
has worn for this last half hour
the look of a tennis umpire
who hates both players.

A forefinger taps morse
on a knee jolting out of time
to the jukebox. The other hand
flexes, rises, hovers –
two fingers shaped like a pistol
shoot forward at a known answer,

bang off the touch-screen.
Half a century since he played
the fruit machines as a lad,
oranges, apples and limes
clacking into place, nudge and hold
making a smidgin of difference

if you were sharp enough,
but really all down to luck
and how much loose change
was an acceptable loss. Pinball
was better: the silver ball,
the buzzers and bells, the slam

of the hip against the machine,
a shop-floor nobody locked
into a fantasy of leather jacket
and Route 66, motorcycle
parked on a dusty strip, Chevys
and Peterbilts and neon signs.

ALL-DAYER

for Alex

We lost our jobs at the same time. Drew our dole
the same day, you at the benefit office near
the station – an ugly, utilitarian building, cold
enough to twin Nottingham with East Berlin circa
John le Carré – me at Sovereign House
in Bulwell, its "job centre" sign more like a joke
at our expense than a statement of purpose.
We signed on early, got out quick, cashed our giros.
By noon we were at the Arboretum Manor.
This was back in the day, before mortgages, loan
repayments and car tax put our finances on the skids.
Food and a couple of pints for under a fiver –
plenty of shrapnel for the pool table; back when
it was twenty pence a game and not a quid.

A couple of hours at the Arbo (as we called it –
we truncated the names of our favourite boozers)
and a few frames was how we started it,
the fortnightly ritual of wasted money: the all-dayer.
We'd walk out onto Arboretum Street and whichever
direction we chose, we kept going in that direction,
one pint in every pub we passed, however
dilapidated it looked, however uninviting.
Fag-burned seats, wallpaper peeling, tables scarred
"Jon 4 Suze", knife-etched? Bad reputation, shitty
dive? Fine by us: broadened the appeal.
It was better than frequenting wine bar
or theme pub. We channelled inverted snobbery,
sneered at such places. We kept it real.

One afternoon in the Vernon, discussing
a TV documentary on Kathleen Ferrier,
we heard a phlegmy, "Classical music? Fuckin'
ponces!" from a corner table. An old codger,
swigging cheap lager from a can to supplement
the barely-touched half pint that sat before
him. You were up and marching over like a shot.
You grabbed him by the neck. I held the door.
He spiralled as you threw him out. A howl
of protest, then: "I had a bag, you fuckers."
It was under the table, contained two cans he'd not
drunk yet. You threw it after him, a fast bowl,
real power behind it, only just missing the luckless
sod. The cans exploded in a wash of froth.

But most of the old boys were good company,
stories worth listening to for the price of a pint.
Tall tales, poetic licence? Didn't matter. One guy,
Merchant Navy, reminisced about the Orient
and opium dens, talked up the proverbial
girl in every port (albeit paid for). A world
tour of vice. The closest *we* came to his lifestyle
was when two working girls on Forest Road
asked if we were looking for business. They
must have been desperate to drum up trade:
anyone could have seen we were wrecked,
barely able to walk a straight line. Your reply:
"Do you give discounts for the unemployed?"
The answer was no – or words to that effect.

The evenings: that's where memory gets foggier:
last orders, last handful of coins, last bus home –
stumble-drunk finales reduced to a blur
or swallowed by those patches of lost time
that didn't worry me enough back then to ease
off the hard stuff, but would scare the hell
out of me now: hastily checking for wallet, keys
and roll call of personal effects. All was well
if you hadn't lost anything and there was no blood.
Waking in your own room, rather than one
with an on-call button for a nurse –
result! Pop two Alka Seltzer, stay in bed,
avoid daylight till the hangover's gone.
No job to get up for. It could have been worse.

OFFER

Buy eight pints and get the ninth free.
Pick up your loyalty card, register online,
offer ends soon. Please drink responsibly.

Follow us on Facebook, upload a selfie
framed to incorporate the pub's sign,
buy eight pints and get the ninth free,

Tweet and re-Tweet #FreePintForMe,
but get them in quick, don't waste time –
the offer ends soon. Please drink responsibly –

we did append that caveat, didn't we?
Drink aware. Stay safe. Please, please don't drive.
Buy eight pints and get the ninth free,

designate a driver, leave your car keys
at home; down those pints, work toward the ninth:
the offer ends soon. Please drink responsibly.

We can't stress that enough. Seriously:
know your limits. Alcohol addiction ruins lives.
Buy eight pints and get the ninth free,
offer ends soon. Please drink responsibly.

IRISH BAR, EAST MIDLANDS

The façade is a study in grim.
Stucco walls, whitewashed a decade ago.
Faded pub sign, rusty hinge. The door's
a slab of dark guarded by a smoker
with a thousand-yard stare. You don't
go in. You don't need to. You know
well enough the bar will be lined
with his type: shaven heads, tattoos,
football shirts, pints swilled from a glass
that looks like a vase. Men who act hard,
talking up the rhetoric of *The Daily Mail*
as their grandfathers gaze down
from a heaven of bitter and barstools
and formica tables, shaking their heads
at the loose change of opinionism
thrown by these men into the begging bowl
of a Facebook post about immigrants;
the hawkings up of men in a Midlands pub
who never came closer to the Emerald Isle
than watching *Hunger* and feeling queasy –
who outside this venue have been known
to slag off "Paddys" and "Micks"
and within it forego Guinness for lager.

CARMELITA

after Warren Zevon

Not heroin but whisky, and Echo Park
is removed from Bestwood Park
by more than a Greyhound ticket
or ten cold hours in a boxcar

but sometimes a place is arrived at
where everything is worn down
to the coarse grain
of what was always going to happen

and the only difference
is whether the song was playing on a radio
scratchy with static in a hotel room
or a museum-piece jukebox in a bar

that serves one brand of beer,
where the few notes
you pawned your iPad for
will cover this drink and maybe the next.

THE LONG DARK CHUCKING-OUT TIME OF THE SOUL

Last orders for redemption
and you were too busy
feeding your existentialism
into a slot machine
that promised a pay-out
in some gelded form.

You were rehearsing
that "stuff your job" speech
in the bathroom mirror,
projecting the boss's face
onto the boxy reflection
of the condom machine.

You took too long sluicing
your hands under the tap,
soaping off the muck
of who you voted for last time
and what you said in anger
when someone called you out

on everything you deny.
The dryer breathed a pittance
of hot air then gave up.
You shrugged, went back in
and they were calling time
on second chances. Now

you're lost and sobering up.
The city is not how it was.
Someone's muted the volume,
detuned the geography.
Walls muscle in. Alleyways
lead back on themselves.

The cabs are driven by ghosts.
Your watch has stopped.
There are names and dates
in street signs and house numbers
that seem to mean something
you can't remember. How many

wrong turns brought you here?

LITANY

The novelty value is irresistible:
a pint and a whisky chaser
in a pub that used to be a chapel.

Stained glass, stone walls. Deconsecrated.
Harsh word – the ecumenical equivalent
of a plane, airworthiness certificate

rescinded, brought to ground,
denied its element. But something
of the godly remains, beyond

mere architecture. The congregration
is different, though. No prayers,
no liturgy, no hymns. Salvation

isn't half-price during Happy Hour.
Anyone looking for a shot
at absolution, a shot of Absolut

is the closest they'll get;
there's one spirit the present owners
aren't licensed to serve. And yet –

despite the crowd of binge-drinkers
giving it the one-up-one-down-one-in-the-air
dexterity of jugglers,

despite the piss-head Romeos with their
lad's magazine chat-up lines
and deodorant commercial *savoir faire*

– something of the godly remains.
Maybe it's in the likenesses
of saints in those imposing windows,

or how the ceiling's high arch dampens
raucous laughter almost to silence.
Or maybe it's the godliness

of funerals, that unshakeable sense
of loss, of solemnity –
like a service of remembrance

for the pubs of my youth.
Dearly beloved, we are gathered here today
in remembrance of the New

Vic, the Newcastle Arms … the litany
begins. The Arboretum Manor,
the Fountain Inn, the Granby,

Byrons, the Bull & Butcher,
Loggerheads, the Dog & Bear,
the Apollo, the Deer Stalker,

the Horse & Jockey, the Goose Fair,
the Scots Grey, the Earl Manvers,
the Old General, the Jester,

the Grove, the Hall Park Tavern,
the Man of Trent, the Golden Ball,
the Belle Vue, the John Barleycorn,

the Langham, Peggers, the Lion Hotel
now an amusement arcade.
Others standing empty, inch-thick steel

bolted over windows. Or torn down to make way
for car parks, retail units, student flats.
Or sadder still demolished entirely,

nothing left but broken glass and weeds
and some guy like me who'll reminisce
about meeting up with mates

and playing pool and getting pissed,
a ritual which defined that half decade
from late teens to early twenties

when the world was yours and getting paid
meant after you passed your mam
a couple of notes for board

the rest was disposable income.
And where better to dispose
of it than down your local? Sink

a few pints, feed the jukebox, cadge a smoke,
swear you'd never end up
like the old guys playing dominoes,

clustered in the corner, half pints sipped
slow, roll-ups from tins. Hindsight
gives them the last laugh. *They* had a pub

that was their local all their lives,
where they congregrated after work
or after the match, where they met their wives

and where their wedding receptions took
place, where they stood their kids
that key-to-the-door birthday drink,

where the good and the bad was shared
and evened out. Where their friends
would choose to gather at the end

and raise a glass and make a toast to them.

LAST ORDERS AT THE JERUSALEM TAVERN

And when last orders were called
he gathered his friends around him
and said unto them:

"Take these, one of you – these
are my car keys which are given to you;
do this in certainty that the evening
will not end in hospital or holding cell,
nor my car end its days in the scrapyard.

"Take this – this is my wallet
which is given to you in the eternal promise
of its return tomorrow, not a single note
the lighter, but having kept me
from distractions on the way home."

One began to ask of him
what was meant by "distractions", but
another answered with a light clip
to the back of the head.

"Take this," he said unto them: "this
is the fight I was going to have
in the car park; and this is the wrong word
that would have provoked it; and these
are the empty macho protocols
which govern the exchange of blows.

"And take these, all of you – these
are my good wishes for the evening,
for soft footfalls over thresholds
and your sleeping families undisturbed,
for brotherhood that does not involve
flags or wargames. Tomorrow,
I will lay my hands upon those of you
who are hungover. Go in peace."